D0915046

The Christian Attitude Towards War

TABOR COLLEGE LIBRARY HILLSBORO, KANSAS

The Words of Christ Commonly Quoted For or Against War.

A Compendium Prepared For Study Groups.

TABOR COLLEGE LIBRARY HILLSBORO, KANSAS

393

7537

CONTENTS

The quotations from the American Edition of the Revised Bible, as printed in this pamphlet, are copyright, 1901, by Thomas Nelson & Sons, and are used by permission.

REPORT

1. Name of Church..

2. Address of Church...

3. Character of study group...

4. Conclusions reached on the three points outlined in the last paragraph of the Introduction. *(Use additional sheets if necessary.)*

(Signed)...Pastor

....Leader

Date...

Detach this page carefully and send to the

COMMISSION ON THE CHURCH AND SOCIAL SERVICE
OF THE FEDERAL COUNCIL OF CHURCHES
105 East 22d Street
New York City

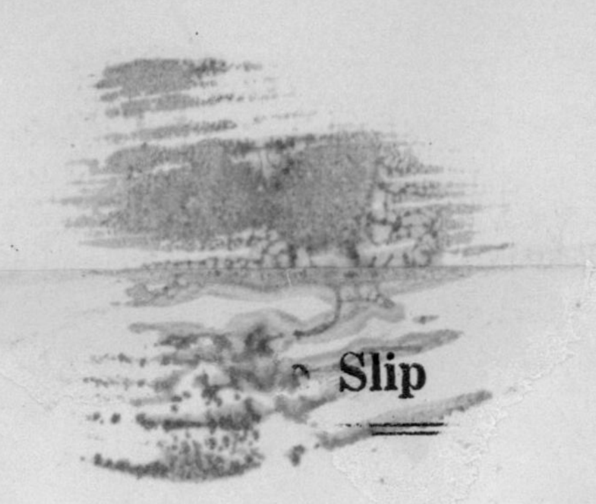
Slip

INTRODUCTION

The Quadrennial Meeting of the Federal Council of Churches, held at Rochester in December, 1928, in discussing a proposed revision of the Social Ideals of the Churches, instructed the Commission on the Church and Social Service to ascertain the mind of the church on the subject of the Christian attitude toward war.

In order to focus the thought of the churches on this matter, it has seemed that nothing could be more pertinent than to present for their consideration the words of Christ commonly quoted for or against war. When the churches discover the mind of Christ in this matter, they will have discovered also the basis for their own convictions and loyalties.

It is suggested, therefore, that various groups in individual churches undertake a serious study of the words and spirit of Christ concerning war. A committee of one of the churches, following a request by the New York Presbytery, drew up the compendium herewith presented and have kindly consented to its use for this study. Each pastor will know which group in his church may be best adapted to undertake and report on such a study. In some churches it will be the Adult Bible Class; in others, the Young People's Society; in others, the pastor may wish to conduct a series of midweek prayer meetings on the subject, drawing those present into discussion, thought and prayer on this matter which is so vital to the spiritual life both of the individual and of society.

The course can probably be covered by the group in six sessions. A competent leader should be provided. The meaning of each passage should be brought out in the light of the context, the historical background, and the circumstances under which the words were spoken.

It should be carefully noted that the chapter headings and subtitles in this pamphlet are of course not intended to be authoritative interpretations of the passages cited, but merely represent the views of those who have commonly quoted the passages in justification of their particular contentions. The group and each individual must come to their own conclusions as to the meaning of Christ.

We have striven to set forth impartially the words of Christ which have been claimed to have a bearing on the subject of war, and to use the minimum of organization necessary to bring together related quotations. It will be observed that the same verses are sometimes cited on opposite sides of the question, while other verses are included which may be considered of doubtful relevancy. A considerable number of verses, it should be pointed out, are extracts from parables, a part of their picture material.

It seemed unwise to eliminate any passages commonly brought forward in the discussion of war and peace, or to comment on the same. We leave it to individual students or groups of students to determine for themselves the value of the passage. We would only call attention to the danger of over-emphasizing letter and verse rather than the spirit of Christ's life and teachings, and would warn our readers against this pitfall. We hope that in the words of Jesus may be found a focusing of His spirit upon this difficult question.

At the close of the careful study of this matter, by whatever group in the church may undertake it, it is requested that a report be made to the Federal Council's Commission on the Church and Social Service, expressing the final understanding of the group: (1) as to the meaning of the words and spirit of Christ in regard to war; (2) whether or not, in the light of these conclusions, the church has a duty with respect to war and peace. Please report also (3) whether your group feels that the Federal Council of Churches should or should not adopt as one of the Social Ideals of the Churches the following resolution, which was presented at the Rochester meeting and referred back to the churches for consideration.

THAT THE CHURCHES STAND FOR:

> The renunciation of war and the refusal of the Church of Christ as an institution to be used as an instrument or an agency in the support of war.

It is requested that reports be sent in as soon as the group has completed the course, if possible within the next months.

COMMISSION ON THE CHURCH AND SOCIAL SERVICE
OF THE FEDERAL COUNCIL OF CHURCHES.

March, 1929

CHAPTER I.

JESUS' ACTS AND TEACHINGS WHICH IT IS CLAIMED JUSTIFY WAR.

1. JESUS IS SAID TO HAVE JUSTIFIED WAR IN PROPHESYING FUTURE WARS.

"And ye shall hear of wars and rumors of wars; see that ye be not troubled: for these things must needs come to pass; but the end is not yet. For nation shall rise against nation, and kingdom against kingdom; and there shall be famines and earthquakes in divers places. But all these things are the beginning of travail."—Matt. 24: 6-8.

(Parallel passages: Mark 13: 7-8; Luke 21: 9-11.)

"And when he drew nigh, he saw the city and wept over it, saying, If thou hadst known in this day, even thou, the things which belong unto peace! but now they are hid from thine eyes. For the days shall come upon thee, when thine enemies shall cast up a bank about thee, and compass thee round, and keep thee in on every side, and shall dash thee to the ground, and thy children within thee; and they shall not leave in thee one stone upon another; because thou knewest not the time of thy visitation."—Luke 19: 41-44.

(Parallel passages: Matt. 24: 2; Mark 13: 2; Luke 21: 6.)

"But when ye see Jerusalem compassed with armies, then know that her desolation is at hand. Then let them that are in Judea flee unto the mountains; and let them that are in the midst of her depart out; and let not them that are in the country enter therein. For these are days of vengeance, that all things which are written may be fulfilled. Woe unto them that are with child and to them that give suck in those days! for there shall be great distress upon the land, and wrath unto this people. And they shall fall by the edge of the sword, and shall be led captive into all the nations: and Jerusalem shall be trodden down of the Gentiles, until the times of the Gentiles be fulfilled."—Luke 21: 20-24.

"And Jesus went out from the temple, and was going on his way; and his disciples came to him to show him the buildings of the temple. But he answered and said unto them, See ye not all these things? verily I say unto you, There shall not be left here one stone upon another, that shall not be thrown down."—Matt. 24: 1-2.

(Parallel passage: Mark 13: 2; Luke 21: 6.)

2. JESUS IS SAID TO HAVE JUSTIFIED WAR IN RECOGNIZING THAT HIS RELIGION WOULD BRING DISSENSION.

"Think not that I came to send peace on the earth: I came not to send peace, but a sword. For I came to set a man at variance against his father, and the daughter against her mother, and the daughter in law against her mother in law: and a man's foes shall be they of his own household."—Matt. 10: 34-36.

"I came to cast fire upon the earth; and what do I desire, if it is already kindled? But I have a baptism to be baptized with; and how am I straitened till it be accomplished! Think ye that I am come to give peace in the earth? I tell you, Nay; but rather division: for there shall be from henceforth five in one house divided, three against two, and two against three. They shall be divided, father against son, and son against father; mother against daughter, and daughter against her mother; mother in law against her daughter in law, and daughter in law against her mother in law."—Luke 12: 49-53.

"Now there went with him great multitudes: and he turned, and said unto them, If any man cometh unto me, and hateth not his own father, and mother, and wife, and children, and brethren and sisters, yea, and his own life also, he cannot be my disciple."—Luke 14: 25-26.

3. JESUS IS SAID TO HAVE JUSTIFIED WAR IN RECOGNIZING THE VALUE OF BEING PREPARED.

"And he said unto them, When I sent you forth without purse, and wallet, and shoes, lacked ye anything? And they said, Nothing. And he said unto them, But now, he that hath a purse, let him take it, and likewise a wallet; and he that hath none, let him sell his cloak, and buy a sword."—Luke 22: 35-36.

"When the strong man fully armed guardeth his own court, his goods are in peace: but when a stronger than he shall come upon him, and overcome him, he taketh from him his whole armor wherein he trusted, and divideth his spoils."—Luke 11: 21-22.
(Parallel passages: Matt. 12: 29; Mark 3: 27.)

"Or what king, as he goeth to encounter another king in war, will not sit down first and take counsel whether he is able with ten thousand to meet him that cometh against him with twenty thousand?"—Luke 14: 31.

"Blessed are those servants, whom the lord when he cometh shall find watching: verily I say unto you, that he shall gird himself, and make them sit down to meat, and shall come and serve them. And if he shall come in the second watch, and if in the third, and find them so, blessed are those servants. But know this, that if the master of the house had known in what hour the thief was coming, he would have watched, and not have left his house to be broken through. Be ye also ready: for in an hour that ye think not the Son of man cometh."—Luke 12: 37-40.

(Parallel passage: Matt. 24: 42-44.)

4. JESUS IS SAID TO HAVE JUSTIFIED WAR IN IMPLYING THAT FORCE IS JUSTIFIABLE UNDER CERTAIN CONDITIONS.

"Pilate answered, Am I a Jew? Thine own nation and the chief priests delivered thee unto me: what hast thou done? Jesus answered, My kingdom is not of this world: if my kingdom were of this world, then would my servants fight, that I should not be delivered to the Jews: but now is my kingdom not from hence."—John 18: 35-36.

"And he began to speak unto them in parables. A man planted a vineyard, and set a hedge about it, and digged a pit for the winepress, and built a tower, and let it out to husbandmen, and went into another country. And at the season he sent to the husbandmen a servant, that he might receive from the husbandmen of the fruits of the vineyard. And they took him, and beat him, and sent him away empty. And again he sent unto them another servant; and him they wounded in the head, and handled shamefully. And he sent another; and him they killed: and many others; beating some, and killing some. He had yet one, a beloved son: he sent him last unto them, saying, They will reverence my son. But those husbandmen said among themselves, This is the heir; come, let us kill him, and the inheritance shall be ours. And they took him, and killed him, and cast him forth out of the vineyard. What therefore will the lord of the vineyard do? he will come and destroy the husbandmen, and will give the vineyard unto others."—Mark 12:1-9.

(Parallel passages: Luke 20:9-16; Matt. 21:33-41.)

"But whoso shall cause one of these little ones that believe on me to stumble, it is profitable for him that a great millstone should be hanged about his neck, and that he should be sunk in the depth of the sea. Woe unto the world because of occasions of stumbling! for it must needs be that the occasions come; but woe to that man through whom the occasion cometh!"—Matt. 18:6-7.

(Parallel passages: Mark 9:42; Luke 17:1-2.)

5. JESUS IS SAID TO HAVE JUSTIFIED WAR IN COMMENDING THE CENTURION, A MAN OF WAR.

"And when he was entered into Capernaum, there came unto him a centurion, beseeching him, and saying, Lord, my servant lieth in the house sick of the palsy, grievously tormented. And he saith unto him, I will come and heal him. And the centurion answered and said, Lord, I am not worthy that thou shouldst come under my roof; but only say the word, and my servant shall be healed. For I also am a man under authority, having under myself soldiers: and I say to this one, Go, and he goeth; and to another, Come, and he cometh; and to my servant, Do this, and he doeth it. And when Jesus heard it, he marvelled, and said to them that followed, Verily I say unto you, "I have not found so great faith, no, not in Israel. And Jesus said unto the centurion, Go thy way; as thou hast believed, so be it done unto thee. And the servant was healed in that hour."—Matt. 8:5-10, 13.

(Parallel passage: Luke 7:1-10.)

6. JESUS IS SAID TO HAVE JUSTIFIED WAR IN ADVOCATING OBEDIENCE TO AUTHORITY.

"And they send unto him certain of the Pharisees and of the Herodians, that they might catch him in talk. And when they were come, they say unto him, Teacher, we know that thou art true, and carest not for any one; for thou regardest not the person of men, but of a truth teachest the way of God: Is it lawful to give tribute unto Caesar, or not? Shall we give, or shall we not give? But he, knowing their hypocrisy, said unto them, Why make ye trial of me? bring me a denarius, that I may see it. And they brought it. And he saith unto them, Whose is this image and superscription? And they said unto him, Caesar's. And Jesus said unto them, Render unto Caesar the things that are Caesar's, and unto God the things that are God's. And they marvelled greatly at him."—Mark 12:13-17.

(Parallel pasages: Matt. 22:15-22; Luke 20:20-26.)

7. JESUS IS SAID TO HAVE JUSTIFIED WAR IN ADVOCATING THE PAYING OF TAXES, KNOWING THAT THEY MIGHT BE USED BY THE ROMAN WAR MACHINE.

"And they send unto him certain of the Pharisees and of the Herodians, that they might catch him in talk. And when they were come, they say unto him, Teacher, we know that thou art true, and carest not for any one; for thou regardest not the person of men, but of a truth teachest the way of God: Is it lawful to give tribute unto Caesar, or not? Shall we give, or shall we not give? But he, knowing their hypocrisy, said unto them, Why make ye trial of me? bring me a denarius, that I may see it. And they brought it. And he saith unto them, Whose is this image and superscription? And they said unto him,

Caesar's. And Jesus said unto them, Render unto Caesar the things that are Caesar's, and unto God the things that are God's. And they marvelled greatly at him."—Mark 12: 13-17.

(Parallel passages: Matt. 22; 15-22; Luke 20: 20-26.)

8. JESUS IS SAID TO HAVE JUSTIFIED WAR IN DEMANDING SELF-SACRIFICE, EVEN TO THE POINT OF DEATH, IN DEFENSE OF VALUES THAT ARE MORE IMPORTANT THAN LIFE.

"And he said unto all, If any man would come after me, let him deny himself, and take up his cross daily, and follow me. For whosoever would save his life shall lose it; but whosoever shall lose his life for my sake, the same shall save it. For what is a man profited, if he gain the whole world, and lose or forfeit his own self?" —Luke 9: 23-25.

(Parallel passages: Matt. 16: 24-26; Mark 8: 34-37.)

"But Jesus called them unto him, and said, Ye know that the rulers of the Gentiles lord it over them, and their great ones exercise authority over them. Not so shall it be among you: but whosoever would become great among you shall be your minister; and whosoever would be first among you shall be your servant: even as the Son of man came not to be ministered unto, but to minister, and to give his life a ransom for many."—Matt. 20: 25-28.

(Parallel passages: Mark 10: 42-45; Mark 9: 35b; Luke 22: 25-26.)

"This is my commandment, that ye love one another even as I have loved you. Greater love hath no man than this, that a man lay down his life for his friends." —John 15: 12-13.

9. JESUS IS SAID TO HAVE JUSTIFIED WAR IN PORTRAYING GOD AS ONE WHO WOULD USE FORCE IN AWARDING PUNISHMENT.

Parable of the unmerciful servant. "Then his lord called him unto him, and saith to him, Thou wicked servant, I forgave thee all that debt, because thou besoughtest me: shouldest not thou also have had mercy on thy fellow-servant, even as I had mercy on thee? And his lord was wroth, and delivered him to the tormentors, till he should pay all that was due. So shall also my heavenly Father do unto you, if ye forgive not every one his brother from your hearts."—Matt. 18: 32-35.

"As therefore the tares are gathered up and burned with fire; so shall it be in the end of the world. The Son of man shall send forth his angels, and they shall gather out of his kingdom all things that cause stumbling, and them that do iniquity, and shall cast them into the furnace of fire: there shall be the weeping and the gnashing of teeth."—Matt. 13: 40-42.

(Similar passage: Matt. 13: 49-50.)

Parable of the pounds. "And he said unto them that stood by, Take away from him the pound, and give it unto him that hath the ten pounds. And they said unto him, Lord, he hath ten pounds. I say unto you that unto every one that hath shall be given; but from him that hath not, even that which he hath shall be taken away from him. But these mine enemies, that would not that I should reign over them, bring hither, and slay them before me."—Luke 19: 24-27.

(Parallel passage: Matt. 25: 14-30.)

Parable of the faithful and unfaithful servants. "The lord of that servant shall come in a day when he expecteth not, and in an hour when he knoweth not, and shall cut him asunder, and appoint his portion with the hypocrites: there shall be the weeping and the gnashing of teeth." —Matt. 24: 50-51.

(Parallel passage: Luke 12: 42-48.)

"And whosoever shall not receive you, nor hear your words, as ye go forth out of that house or that city, shake off the dust of your feet. Verily I say unto you, It shall be more tolerable for the land of Sodom and Gomorrah in the day of judgment, than for that city."—Matt. 10: 14-15.

"I say unto you, It shall be more tolerable in that day for Sodom, than for that city. Woe unto thee, Chorazin! woe unto thee, Bethsaida! for if the mighty works had been done in Tyre and Sidon, which were done in you, they would have repented long ago, sitting in sackcloth and ashes. But it shall be more tolerable for Tyre and Sidon in the judgment, than for you. And thou, Capernaum, shalt thou be exalted unto heaven? thou shalt be brought down unto Hades."—Luke 10: 12-15.

"But immediately after the tribulation of those days the sun shall be darkened, and the moon shall not give her light, and the stars shall fall from heaven, and the powers of the heavens shall be shaken: and then shall appear the sign of the Son of man in heaven: and then shall all the tribes of the earth mourn, and they shall see the Son of man coming on the clouds of heaven with power and great glory. And he shall send forth his angels with a great sound of a trumpet, and they shall gather together his elect from the four winds, from one end of heaven to the other."—Matt. 24:29-31.

(Parallel passages: Mark 13:24-27; Luke 21:27-28.)

10. JESUS IS SAID TO HAVE JUSTIFIED WAR IN USING FORCE TO DRIVE THE MONEY-CHANGERS FROM THE TEMPLE.

"And the passover of the Jews was at hand, and Jesus went up to Jerusalem. And he found in the temple those that sold oxen and sheep and doves, and the changers of money sitting: and he made a scourge of cords, and cast all out of the temple, both the sheep and the oxen; and he poured out the changers' money, and overthrew their tables; and to them that sold the doves he said, Take these things hence; make not my Father's house a house of merchandise."—John 2:13-16.

(Parallel passages: Matt. 21:12-13; Mark 11:15-17; Luke 19:45-46.)

A Brief of Chapter I.

JESUS' ACTS AND TEACHINGS WHICH IT IS CLAIMED JUSTIFY WAR.

1. *Jesus is said to have justified war in prophesying future wars.*

   Matt. 24:6-8. Parallel passages: Mark 13:7-8; Luke 21:9-11.

   Luke 19:41-44. Parallel passages: Matt. 24:2; Mark 13:2; Luke 21:6.

   Luke 21:20-24.

   Matt. 24:1-2. Parallel passages: Mark 13:2; Luke 21:6.

2. *Jesus is said to have justified war in recognizing that his religion would bring dissension.*

   Matt. 10:34-36.
   Luke 12:49-53.
   Luke 14:25-26.

3. *Jesus is said to have justified war in recognizing the value of being prepared.*

   Luke 22:35-36.
   Luke 11:21-22. Parallel passages: Matt. 12:29; Mark 3:27.
   Luke 14:31.
   Luke 12:37-40. Parallel passage: Matt. 24:42-44.

4. *Jesus is said to have justified war in implying that force is justifiable under certain conditions.*

   John 18:35-36.
   Mark 12:1-9. Parallel passages: Luke 20:9-16; Matt. 21:33-41.
   Matt. 18:6-7. Parallel passages: Mark 9:42; Luke 17:1-2.

5. *Jesus is said to have justified war in commending the Centurion, a man of war.*

   Matt. 8:5-10, 13. Parallel passage: Luke 7:1-10.

6. *Jesus is said to have justified war in advocating obedience to authority.*

   Mark 12:13-17. Parallel passages: Matt. 22:15-22; Luke 20:20-26.

7. *Jesus is said to have justified war in advocating the paying of taxes, knowing that they might be used by the Roman war machine.*

   Mark 12:13-17. Parallel passages; Matt. 22:15-22; Luke 20:20-26.

8. *Jesus is said to have justified war in demanding self-sacrifice, even to the point of death, in defense of values that are more important than life.*

   Luke 9:23-25. Parallel passages: Matt. 16:24-26; Mark 8:34-37.

   Matt. 20:25-28. Parallel passages: Mark 10:42-45; Mark 9:35b; Luke 22:25-26.

   John 15:12-13.

9. *Jesus is said to have justified war in portraying God as one who would use force in awarding punishment.*

   Matt. 18:23-35.

   Matt. 13:40-42. Similar passage: Matt. 13:49-50.

   Luke 19:11-27. Parallel passage: Matt. 25:14-30.

   Matt. 24:45-51. Parallel passage: Luke 12:42-48.

   Matt. 10:14-15.

   Luke 10:10-15.

   Matt. 24:29-31. Parallel passages: Mark 13:24-27; Luke 21:27-28.

10. *Jesus is said to have justified war in using force to drive the moneychangers from the Temple.*

   John 2:13-16. Parallel passages: Matt. 21:12-13; Mark 11:15-17; Luke 19:45-46.

CHAPTER II.

JESUS' ACTS AND TEACHINGS WHICH IT IS CLAIMED CONDEMN WAR

1. JESUS IS SAID TO HAVE CONDEMNED WAR IN REJECTING THE PHILOSOPHY, USED IN DEFENSE OF WAR, THAT THE END JUSTIFIES THE MEANS.

A. *He refused to accept the complete success of his mission secured by compromise with evil.*

"Then was Jesus led up of the Spirit into the wilderness to be tempted of the devil. And when he had fasted forty days and forty nights, he afterward hungered. And the tempter came and said unto him, If thou art the Son of God, command that these stones become bread. But he answered and said, It is written, Man shall not live by bread alone, but by every word that proceedeth out of the mouth of God. Then the devil taketh him into the holy city; and he set him on the pinnacle of the temple, and saith unto him, if thou art the Son of God, cast thyself down: for it is written, He shall give his angels charge concerning thee: and, on their hands they shall bear thee up, lest haply thou dash thy foot against a stone. Jesus said unto him, Again it is written, Thou shalt not make trial of the Lord thy God. Again, the devil taketh him unto an exceeding high mountain, and showeth him all the kingdoms of the world, and the glory of them; and he said unto him, All these things will I give thee, if thou wilt fall down and worship me. Then saith Jesus unto him, Get thee hence, Satan: for it is written, Thou shalt worship the Lord thy God, and him only shalt thou

TABOR COLLEGE LIBRARY HILLSBORO, KANSAS

serve. Then the devil leaveth him; and behold, angels came and ministered unto him."—Matt. 4: 1-11.

(Parallel passages: Mark 1: 12-13; Luke 4: 1-13.)

B. *He forbade resisting evil with evil.*

"Ye have heard that it was said, An eye for an eye, and a tooth for a tooth: but I say unto you, Resist not him that is evil: but whosoever smiteth thee on thy right cheek, turn to him the other also. And if any man would go to law with thee, and take away thy coat, let him have thy cloak also. And whosoever shall compel thee to go one mile, go with him two. Give to him that asketh thee, and from him that would borrow of thee turn not thou away."—Matt. 5: 38-42.

(Parallel passage: Luke 6: 29-30.)

C. *He rejected the law demanding the execution of the criminal for the benefit of society.*

The woman taken in adultery. "Now in the law Moses commanded us to stone such: what then sayest thou of her? And this they said, trying him, that they might have whereof to accuse him. But Jesus stooped down, and with his finger wrote on the ground . . . And Jesus lifted up himself, and said unto her, Woman, where are they? did no man condemn thee? And she said, No man, Lord. And Jesus said, Neither do I condemn thee: go thy way; from henceforth sin no more."—John 8: 5-6, 10-11.

2. JESUS IS SAID TO HAVE CONDEMNED WAR IN SUBSTITUTING THE GOSPEL OF LOVE AS THE WAY OF LIFE.

A. *Beginning with the Beatitudes He extolled all the anti-war virtues: meekness, mercifulness and peace-making.*

"And he opened his mouth and taught them, saying, Blessed are the poor in spirit: for theirs is the kingdom of heaven. Blessed are they that mourn: for they shall be comforted. Blessed are the meek: for they shall inherit the earth. Blessed are they that hunger and thirst after righteousness: for they shall be filled. Blessed are the merciful: for they shall obtain mercy. Blessed are the pure in heart: for they shall see God. Blessed are the peacemakers: for they shall be called sons of God. Blessed are they that have been persecuted for righteousness' sake: for theirs is the kingdom of heaven. Blessed are ye when men shall reproach you, and persecute you, and say all manner of evil against you falsely, for my sake. Rejoice, and be exceeding glad: for great is your reward in heaven: for so persecuted they the prophets that were before you."—Matt. 5: 2-12.

B. *He demanded love of one's racial foes and enemies.*

"But I say unto you that hear, Love your enemies, do good to them that hate you, bless them that curse you, pray for them that despitefully use you. To him that smiteth thee on the one cheek offer also the other; and from him that taketh away thy cloak withhold not thy coat also. Give to every one that asketh thee; and of him that taketh away thy goods ask them not again. And as ye would that men should do to you, do ye also to them likewise. And if ye love them that love you, what thank have ye? for even sinners love those that love them. And if ye do good to them that do good to you, what thank have ye? for even sinners do the same. And if ye lend to them of whom ye hope to receive, what thank have ye? even sinners lend to sinners, to receive again as much. But love your enemies, and do them good, and lend, never despairing; and your reward shall be great, and ye shall be Sons of the Most High: for he is kind toward the unthankful and evil. Be ye merciful, even as your

Father is merciful. And judge not, and ye shall not be judged: and condemn not, and ye shall not be condemned: release, and ye shall be released: give, and it shall be given unto you; good measure, pressed down, shaken together, running over, shall they give into your bosom. For with what measure ye mete it shall be measured to you again."—Luke 6: 27-38.

(Parallel passage: Matt, 5: 43-48.)

C. *He demanded that evil be overcome with good.*

"Ye have heard that it was said, An eye for an eye, and a tooth for a tooth: but I say unto you, Resist not him that is evil: but whosoever smiteth thee on thy right cheek, turn to him the other also. And if any man would go to law with thee, and take away thy coat, let him have thy cloak also. And whosoever shall compel thee to go one mile, go with him two. Give to him that asketh thee, and from him that would borrow of thee turn not thou away. Ye have heard that it was said, Thou shalt love thy neighbor, and hate thine enemy: but I say unto you, Love your enemies, and pray for them that persecute you; that ye may be sons of your Father who is in heaven: for he maketh his sun to rise on the evil and the good, and sendeth rain on the just and the unjust. For if ye love them that love you, what reward have ye? do not even the publicans the same? And if ye salute your brethren only, what do ye more than others? do not even the Gentiles the same? Ye therefore shall be perfect as your heavenly Father is perfect."—Matt. 5: 38-48.

(Parallel passage: Luke 6: 27-38.)

"All things therefore whatsoever ye would that men should do unto you, even so do ye also unto them: for this is the law and the prophets."—Matt. 7: 12.

(Parallel passage: Luke 6: 31.)

D. *He called for arbitration and conciliation in the settling of disputes.*

"If therefore thou art offering thy gift at the altar, and there rememberest that thy brother hath aught against thee, leave there thy gift before the altar, and go thy way, first be reconciled to thy brother, and then come and offer thy gift. Agree with thine adversary quickly, while thou art with him in the way; lest haply the adversary deliver thee to the judge, and the judge deliver thee to the officer, and thou be cast into prison."—Matt. 5: 23-25.

"And if thy brother sin against thee, go, show him his fault between thee and him alone: if he hear thee, thou hast gained thy brother. But if he hear thee not, take with thee one or two more, that at the mouth of two witnesses or three every word may be established. And if he refuse to hear them, tell it unto the church: and if he refuse to hear the church also, let him be unto thee as the Gentile and the publican."—Matt. 18: 15-17.

E. *He ordered nonresistance of evil.*

"But I say unto you, Resist not him that is evil." —Matt. 5: 39.

(Parallel passage: Luke 6: 29.)

"But when they persecute you in this city, flee into the next."—Matt. 10: 23a.

F. *He commanded forgiveness of one's enemies.*

"Then came Peter and said to him, Lord, how oft shall my brother sin against me, and I forgive him? until seven times? Jesus saith unto him, I say not unto thee, until seven times; but, Until seventy times seven."—Matt. 18: 21-22.

"And forgive us our debts, as we also have forgiven our debtors."—Matt. 6: 12.

"Take heed to yourselves: if thy brother sin, rebuke him; and if he repent, forgive him."—Luke 17: 3.

"And whensoever ye stand praying, forgive, if ye have aught against any one; that your Father also who is in heaven may forgive you your trespasses."—Mark 11: 25.

G. *He urged His disciples to live peaceful lives.*

"Go your ways; behold, I send you forth as lambs in the midst of wolves."—Luke 10: 3.

"Behold, I send you forth as sheep in the midst of wolves: be ye therefore wise as serpents, and harmless as doves."—Matt. 10: 16.

H. *He advocated universal brotherhood.*

"This is the great and first commandment. And a second like unto it is this, Thou shalt love thy neighbor as thyself."—Matt. 22: 38-39.

(Parallel passages: Mark 12: 31; Luke 10: 27.)

The good Samaritan. "But a certain Samaritan, as he journeyed, came where he was: and when he saw him, he was moved with compassion, and came to him, and bound up his wounds, pouring on them oil and wine; and he set him on his own beast, and brought him to an inn, and took care of him. . . . Which of these three, thinkest thou, proved neighbor unto him that fell among the robbers? And he said, He that showed mercy on him. And Jesus said unto him, Go, and do thou likewise." —Luke 10: 33, 34, 36, 37.

"A new commandment I give unto you, that ye love one another; even as I have loved you, that ye also love one another. By this shall all men know that ye are my disciples, if ye have love one to another."—John 13: 34-35.

"These things I command you, that ye may love one another."—John 15: 17.

3. JESUS IS SAID TO HAVE CONDEMNED WAR IN FORBIDDING WHATEVER WAS INCONSISTENT WITH THE GOSPEL OF LOVE.

A. *He forbade killing, attempts to kill and even the inner set of a man's will that allowed killing.*

"And behold, one came to him and said, Teacher, what good thing shall I do, that I may have eternal life? And he said unto him, Why askest thou me concerning that which is good? One there is who is good: but if thou wouldest enter into life, keep the commandments. He saith unto him. Which? and Jesus said, Thou shalt not kill."—Matt. 19: 16-18.

(Parallel passages: Mark 10: 17-19; Luke 18: 18-20.)

"And Jesus said unto him, Friend, do that for which thou art come. Then they came and laid hands on Jesus, and took him. And behold, one of them that were with Jesus stretched out his hand, and drew his sword, and smote the servant of the high priest, and struck off his ear. Then saith Jesus unto him, Put up again thy sword into its place: for all they that take the sword shall perish with the sword."—Matt. 26: 50-52.

(Parallel passages: Luke 22: 49-51; John 18: 4-11.)

B. *He warned against selfishness, anger and covetousness.*

"Ye have heard that it was said to them of old time, Thou shalt not kill; and whosoever shall kill shall be in danger of the judgment: but I say unto you, that every one who is angry with his brother shall be in danger of the judgment; and whosoever shall say to his brother, Raca, shall be in danger of the council; and whosoever shall say, Thou fool, shall be in danger of the hell of fire."—Matt. 5: 21-22.

"Lay not up for yourselves treasures upon the earth, where moth and rust consume, and where thieves break through and steal: but lay up for yourselves treasures in heaven, where neither moth nor rust doth consume, and where thieves do not break through nor steal: for where thy treasure is, there will thy heart be also. The lamp of the body is the eye: if therefore thine eye be single, thy whole body shall be full of light. But if thine eye be evil, thy whole body shall be full of darkness. If therefore the light that is in thee be darkness, how great is the darkness! No man can serve two masters: for either he will hate the one, and love the other; or else he will hold to one, and despise the other. Ye cannot serve God and mammon."—Matt. 6: 19-24.

"And one out of the multitude said unto him, Teacher, bid my brother divide the inheritance with me. But he said unto him, Man, who made me a judge or a divider over you? And he said unto them, Take heed and keep yourselves from all covetousness: for a man's life consisteth not in the abundance of the things which he possesseth. And he spake a parable unto them, saying, The ground of a certain rich man brought forth plentifully: and he reasoned within himself, saying, What shall I do because I have not where to bestow my fruits? And he said, This will I do: I will pull down my barns, and build greater; and there will I bestow all my grain and my goods. And I will say to my soul, Soul, thou hast much goods laid up for many years; take thine ease, eat, drink, be merry. But God said unto him, Thou foolish one, this night is thy soul required of thee; and the things which thou hast prepared, whose shall they be? So is he that layeth up treasure for himself, and is not rich toward God."—Luke 12: 13-21.

C. *He condemned reprisals.*

"Ye have heard that it was said, An eye for an eye, and a tooth for a tooth: but I say unto you, Resist not him that is evil."—Matt. 5:38-39a.

"And it came to pass, when the days were well nigh come that he should be received up, he steadfastly set his face to go to Jerusalem, and sent messengers before his face: and they went, and entered into a village of the Samaritans, to make ready for him. And they did not receive him, because his face was as though he were going to Jerusalem. And when his disciples James and John saw this, they said, Lord, wilt thou that we bid fire to come down from heaven, and consume them? But he turned, and rebuked them. And they went to another village."—Luke 9:51-56.

4. JESUS IS SAID TO HAVE CONDEMNED WAR IN PRACTICING WHAT HE PREACHED.

A. *He did not resist his enemies.*

"And while he yet spake, lo, Judas, one of the twelve, came, and with him a great multitude with swords and staves, from the chief priests and elders of the people. Now he that betrayed him gave them a sign, saying, Whomsoever I shall kiss, that is he: take him. And straightway he came to Jesus, and said, Hail, Rabbi; and kissed him. And Jesus said unto him, Friend, do that for which thou art come. Then they came and laid hands on Jesus, and took him. And behold, one of them that were with Jesus stretched out his hand, and drew his sword, and smote the servant of the high priest, and struck off his ear. Then saith Jesus unto him, Put up again thy sword into its place: for all they that take the sword shall perish with the sword. Or thinkest thou that I cannot beseech my Father, and he shall even now send me more than twelve legions of angels? How then should the scriptures be fulfilled, that thus it must be? In that hour said Jesus to the multitudes, Are ye come out as against a robber with swords and staves to seize me? I sat daily in the temple teaching, and ye took me not. But all this is come to pass, that the scriptures of the prophets might be fulfilled. Then all the disciples left him, and fled."—Matt. 26:47-56.

(Parallel passages: Mark 14:43-50; Luke 22:47-54.)

"And the high priest stood up in the midst, and asked Jesus, saying, Answerest thou nothing? what is it which these witness against thee? But he held his peace, and answered nothing . . . And some began to spit on him, and to cover his face, and to buffet him, and to say unto him, Prophesy: and the officers received him with blows of their hands."—Mark 14:60-61a, 65.

(Parallel passage: Matt. 26:62-63. 67-68.)

"And Pilate asked him, Art thou the King of the Jews? And he answering saith unto him, Thou sayest. And the chief priests accused him of many things. And Pilate again asked him, saying, Answerest thou nothing? behold how many things they accuse thee of. But Jesus no more answered anything; insomuch that Pilate marvelled." —Mark 15:2-5.

"Then the soldiers of the Governor took Jesus into the Praetorium, and gathered unto him the whole band.

And they stripped him, and put on him a scarlet robe. And they platted a crown of thorns and put it upon his head, and a reed in his right hand; and they kneeled down before him, and mocked him, saying, Hail, King of the Jews! And they spat upon him, and took the reed and smote him on the head. And when they had mocked him, they took off from him the robe, and put on him his garments, and led him away to crucify him."—Matt. 27:27-31.

(Parallel passage: Mark 15: 16-20.)

B. *He forgave his enemies and loved them.*

"And Jesus said, Father, forgive them; for they know not what they do."—Luke 23:34.

C. *He rebuked Peter for using the sword.*

"Then saith Jesus unto him (Peter), Put up again thy sword into its place: for all they that take the sword shall perish with the sword."—Matt. 26:52.

D. *He refused kingship based on force.*

"Jesus therefore perceiving that they were about to come and take him by force, to make him king, withdrew again into the mountain himself alone."—John 6:15.

E. *He accepted the cross while explaining that his action was a choice, not necessity.*

"From that time began Jesus to show unto his disciples, that he must go unto Jerusalem, and suffer many things of the elders and chief priests and scribes, and be killed, and the third day be raised up. And Peter took him, and began to rebuke him, saying, Be it far from

thee, Lord: this shall never be unto thee. But he turned, and said unto Peter, Get thee behind me, Satan: thou art a stumbling-block unto me: for thou mindest not the things of God, but the things of men."—Matt. 16:21-23.
(Parallel passages: Mark 8:31-33; Luke 9:22.)

"Then they came and laid hands on Jesus, and took him. And behold, one of them that were with Jesus stretched out his hand, and drew his sword, and smote the servant of the high priest, and struck off his ear. Then saith Jesus unto him, Put up again thy sword in its place: for all they that take the sword shall perish with the sword. Or thinkest thou that I cannot beseech my Father, and he shall even now send me more than twelve legions of angels?"—Matt. 26:50b-53.

F. *He broke down racial and national prejudices by His own example.*

"And Jesus went out thence, and withdrew into the parts of Tyre and Sidon. And behold, a Canaanitish woman came out from those borders, and cried, saying, Have mercy on me, O Lord, thou son of David; my daughter is grievously vexed with a demon. . . . Then Jesus answered and said unto her, O woman, great is thy faith; be it done unto thee even as thou wilt. And her daughter was healed from that hour."—Matt. 15:21-22, 28.

(Parallel passage: Mark 7:24-30.)

The Samaritan woman. "There cometh a woman of Samaria to draw water: Jesus saith unto her, Give me to drink. . . . Woman, believe me, the hour cometh, when neither in this mountain, nor in Jerusalem, shall ye worship the Father. . . . God is a Spirit: and they that worship him must worship in spirit and truth."—John 4:7, 21b-24.

The commended centurion. "And when he was entered into Capernaum, there came unto him a centurion, beseeching him. . . . And when Jesus heard it, he marvelled, and said to them that followed, Verily I say unto you, I have not found so great faith, no, not in Israel. And I say unto you, that many shall come from the east and the west, and shall sit down with Abraham and Isaac, and Jacob in the Kingdom of Heaven. . . . And Jesus said unto the centurion, Go thy way; as thou hast believed, so be it done unto thee."—Matt. 8:5, 10-11, 13.

(Parallel passage: Luke 7:1-10.)

5. JESUS IS SAID TO HAVE CONDEMNED WAR IN DEMANDING THAT HIS FOLLOWERS PRACTICE THE WAY OF LOVE THAT HE PREACHED.

A. *He proclaimed the Great Commandment. Can one love his neighbor as himself and make war against him?*

"Teacher, which is the great commandment in the law? And he said unto him, Thou shalt love the Lord thy God with all thy heart, and with all thy soul, and with all thy mind. This is the great and first commandment. And a second like unto it is this, Thou shalt love thy neighbor as thyself. On these two commandments the whole law hangeth, and the prophets."—Matt. 22:36-40.

(Parallel passages: Mark 12:28-31; Luke 10:25-38.)

B. *He required the observance of the Golden Rule*

"All things therefore whatsoever ye would that men should do unto you, even so do ye also unto them: for this is the law and the prophets."—Matt. 7:12.

(Parallel passage: Luke 6:31.)

C. *He commanded that we live lives of service to all.*

"But Jesus called them unto him, and said, Ye know that the rulers of the Gentiles lord it over them, and their great ones exercise authority over them. Not so shall it be among you: but whosoever would become great among you shall be your minister; and whosoever would be first among you shall be your servant: even as the Son of man came not to be ministered unto, but to minister and to give his life a ransom for many."—Matt. 20: 25-28.

(Parallel passages: Mark 10: 42-45; Luke 22: 25-26.)

"So when they had broken their fast, Jesus saith to Simon Peter, Simon, son of John, lovest thou me more than these? He saith unto him, Yea, Lord; thou knowest that I love thee. He saith unto him, Feed my lambs. He saith to him again a second time, Simon, son of John, lovest thou me? He saith unto him, Yea, Lord; thou knowest that I love thee. He saith unto him, Tend my sheep. He saith unto him the third time, Simon, son of John, lovest thou me? Peter was grieved because he said unto him the third time, Lovest thou me? And he said unto him, Lord, thou knowest all things; thou knowest that I love thee. Jesus saith unto him, Feed my sheep."—John 21: 15-17.

"Then shall the King say unto them on his right hand, Come, ye blessed of my Father, inherit the kingdom prepared for you from the foundation of the world: for I was hungry, and ye gave me to eat; I was thirsty, and ye gave me drink; I was a stranger, and ye took me in; naked, and ye clothed me; I was sick, and ye visited me; I was in prison, and ye came unto me. Then shall the righteous answer him, saying, Lord, when saw we thee hungry, and fed thee? or athirst, and gave thee drink? And when saw we thee a stranger, and took thee in? or naked, and clothed thee? And when saw we thee sick, or in prison, and came unto thee? And the King shall answer and say unto them, Verily I say unto you, Inasmuch as ye did it unto one of these my brethren, even these least, ye did it unto me."—Matt. 25: 34-40.

D. *He required the life of self-sacrifice as a test of discipleship.*

"And he called unto him the multitude with his disciples, and said unto them, If any man would come after me, let him deny himself, and take up his cross, and follow me. For whosoever would save his life shall lose it; and whosoever shall lose his life for my sake and the gospel's shall save it. For what doth it profit a man, to gain the whole world, and forfeit his life? For what should a man give in exchange for his life? For whosoever shall be ashamed of me and of my words in this adulterous and sinful generation, the Son of man also shall be ashamed of him, when he cometh in the glory of his Father with the holy angels."—Mark 8: 34-38.

(Parallel passages: Matt. 16: 24-26; Luke 9: 23-25.)

"This is my commandment, that ye love one another, even as I have loved you. Greater love hath no man than this, that a man lay down his life for his friends."—John 15: 12-13.

E. *He required a life of supreme loyalty to God.*

"And Jesus answered and said unto him, It is written, Thou shalt worship the Lord thy God, and him only shalt thou serve."—Luke 4:8.

(Parallel passage: Matt. 4: 10.)

"Teacher, which is the great commandment in the law? And he said unto him, Thou shalt love the Lord thy God with all thy heart, and with all thy soul, and with all thy mind."—Matt. 22: 36-37.

(Parallel passage: Mark 12: 28-31.)

6. JESUS IS SAID TO HAVE CONDEMNED WAR IN REVEALING GOD AS A UNIVERSAL FATHER.

A. *He revealed Him as a loving Father.*

"For God so loved the world, that he gave his only begotten Son, that whosoever believeth on him should not perish, but have eternal life."—John 3: 16.

"That ye may be sons of your Father who is in heaven: for he maketh his sun to rise on the evil and the good, and sendeth rain on the just and the unjust."—Matt. 5: 45.

"And of which of you that is a father shall his son ask a loaf, and he give him a stone? or a fish, and he for a fish give him a serpent? Or if he shall ask an egg, will he give him a scorpion? If ye then, being evil, know how to give good gifts unto your children, how much more shall your Heavenly Father give the Holy Spirit to them that ask him?"—Luke 11: 11-13.

"I say unto you, that even so there shall be joy in heaven over one sinner that repenteth, more than over ninety and nine righteous persons, who need no repentance. . . . Even so, I say unto you, there is joy in the presence of the angels of God over one sinner that repenteth."—Luke 15: 7, 10.

B. *He portrayed Him as a forgiving Father.*

Parable of the prodigal son. "And he arose, and came to his father. But while he was yet afar off, his father saw him, and was moved with compassion, and ran, and fell on his neck, and kissed him. . . . But the father said to his servants, Bring forth quickly the best robe, and put it on him; and put a ring on his hand, and shoes on his feet: and bring the fatted calf, and kill it, and let us eat, and make merry: . . . But it was meet to make merry and be glad: for this thy brother was dead, and is alive again; and was lost, and is found."—Luke 15: 20, 22, 23, 32.

Parable of the pharisee and the publican. "But the publican, standing afar off, would not lift up so much as his eyes unto heaven, but smote his breast, saying, God, be thou merciful to me a sinner. I say unto you, This man went down to his house justified rather than the other: for every one that exalteth himself shall be humbled; but he that humbleth himself shall be exalted."—Luke 18: 13-14.

"For if ye forgive men their trespasses, your heavenly Father will also forgive you."—Matt. 6: 14.

C. *He asserted that He was a redeeming Father.*

"And as Moses lifted up the serpent in the wilderness, even so must the Son of man be lifted up; that whosoever believeth may in him have eternal life. For God so loved the world, that he gave his only begotten Son, that whosoever believeth on him should not perish, but have eternal life. For God sent not the Son into the world to judge the world; but that the world should be saved through him."—John 3: 14-17.

"How think ye? if any man have a hundred sheep, and one of them be gone astray, doth he not leave the ninety and nine, and go unto the mountains, and seek that which goeth astray? And if so be that he find it, verily I say unto you, he rejoiceth over it more than over the ninety and nine which have not gone astray. Even so it is not the will of your Father who is in heaven, that one of these little ones should perish."—Matt. 18: 12-14.

7. JESUS IS SAID TO HAVE CONDEMNED WAR IN ASSERTING THAT THE INDIVIDUAL IS OF INFINITE VALUE.

"And he said unto them, What man shall there be of you, that shall have one sheep, and if this fall into a pit on the sabbath day, will he not lay hold on it, and lift it out? How much then is a man of more value than a sheep!"—Matt. 12:11-12.

"Are not five sparrows sold for two pence? and not one of them is forgotten in the sight of God. But the very hairs of your head are all numbered. Fear not: ye are of more value than many sparrows."—Luke 12:6-7.

(Parallel passage: Matt. 10:29-31.)

"Consider the ravens, that they sow not, neither reap; which have no store-chamber nor barn; and God feedeth them: of how much more value are ye than the birds!"—Luke 12:24.

"And the King shall answer and say unto them, Verily I say unto you, Inasmuch as ye did it unto one of these my brethren, even these least, ye did it unto me."—Matt. 25:40.

8. JESUS IS SAID TO HAVE CONDEMNED WAR IN CALLING FOR A RICH AND ABUNDANT LIFE FOR ALL.

"I came that they may have life, and may have it abundantly."—John 10:10b.

9. JESUS IS SAID TO HAVE CONDEMNED WAR IN ESTABLISHING STANDARDS BY WHICH INSTITUTIONS, SUCH AS WAR, MUST BE JUDGED.

"Beware of false prophets, who come to you in sheep's clothing, but inwardly are ravening wolves. By their fruits ye shall know them. Do men gather grapes of thorns, or figs of thistles? Even so every good tree bringeth forth good fruit; but the corrupt tree bringeth forth evil fruit. A good tree cannot bring forth evil fruit, neither can a corrupt tree bring forth good fruit. Every tree that bringeth not forth good fruit is hewn down, and cast into the fire. Therefore by their fruits ye shall know them."—Matt. 7:15-20.

(Parallel passage: Luke 6:43-44.)

A Brief of Chapter II.

JESUS' ACTS AND TEACHINGS WHICH IT IS CLAIMED CONDEMN WAR.

1. *Jesus is said to have condemned war in rejecting the philosophy, used in defense of war, that the end justifies the means.*
   - A. He refused to accept the complete success of his mission secured by compromise with evil.
     Matt. 4:1-11. Parallel passages: Mark 1:12-13; Luke 4:1-13.
   - B. He forbade resisting evil with evil.
     Matt. 5:38-42. Parallel passage: Luke 6:29-30.
   - C. He rejected the law demanding execution of the criminal for the benefit of society.
     John 8:1-11.

2. *Jesus is said to have condemned war in substituting the Gospel of Love as the way of life.*
   - A. Beginning with the Beatitudes He extolled all the anti-war virtues; meekness, mercifulness, and peace-making.
     Matt. 5:2-12.
   - B. He demanded love of one's racial foes and enemies.
     Luke 6:27-38. Parallel passage: Matt. 5:43-48.

TABOR COLLEGE LIBRARY
HILLSBORO KANSAS 67063

C. He demanded that evil be overcome with good.
Matt. 5: 38-48. Parallel passage: Luke 6: 27-38.
Matt. 7: 12. Parallel passage: Luke 6: 31.

D. He called for arbitration and conciliation in the settling of disputes.
Matt. 5: 23-25.
Matt. 18: 15-17.

E. He ordered nonresistance of evil.
Matt. 5: 39. Parallel passage: Luke 6: 29.
Matt. 10: 23a.

F. He advocated forgiveness of one's enemies.
Matt. 18: 21-22.
Matt. 6: 12.
Luke 17: 3.
Mark 11: 25.

G. He urged His disciples to live peaceful lives.
Luke 10: 3.
Matt. 10: 16.

H. He advocated universal brotherhood.
Matt. 22: 38-39. Parallel passages: Mark 12: 31; Luke 10: 27.
Luke 10: 25-37.
John 13: 34-35.
John 15: 17.

3. *Jesus is said to have condemned war in forbidding whatever was inconsistent with the Gospel of Love.*

A. He forbade killing, attempts to kill and even the inner set of a man's mind that allowed killing.
Matt. 19: 16-18. Parallel passages Mark 10: 17-19; Luke 18: 18-20.
Matt. 26: 50-52. Parallel passages Luke 22: 49-51; John 18: 4-11.

B. He warned against anger, selfishness, and covetousness.
   Matt. 5: 21-22.
   Matt. 6: 19-24.
   Luke 12: 13-21.

C. He condemned reprisals.
   Matt. 5: 38-39a.
   Luke 9: 51-56.

4. *Jesus is said to have condemned war in practicing what he preached.*

A. He did not resist his enemies.
   Matt. 26: 47-56. Parallel passages: Mark 14: 43-50; Luke 22: 47-54.
   Mark 14: 60-65. Parallel passage: Matt. 26: 62-68.
   Mark 15: 2-5.
   Matt. 27: 27-31. Parallel passage: Mark 15: 16-20.

B. He forgave his enemies and loved them.
   Luke 23: 34.

C. He rebuked Peter for using the sword.
   Matt. 26: 52.

D. He refused kingship based on force.
   John 6: 15.

E. He accepted the cross while explaining that his action was a choice, not necessity.
   Matt. 16: 21-23. Parallel passages: Mark 8: 31-33; Luke 9: 22.

F. He broke down racial and national prejudices by his own example.
   Matt. 15:21-28. Parallel passage: Mark 7:24-30.

John 4: 5-42.
Matt. 8: 5-13. Parallel passage: Luke 7: 1-10.

5. *Jesus is said to have condemned war in demanding that his followers practice the way of love that he preached.*

A. He proclaimed the Great Commandment. Can one love his neighbor as himself and make war against him?
Matt. 22: 36-40. Parallel passages Mark 12: 28-31; Luke 10: 25-38.

B. He required the observance of the Golden Rule.
Matt. 7: 12. Parallel passage Luke 6: 31.

C. He commanded that we live lives of service to all.
Matt. 30: 25-28. Parallel passages: Mark 10: 42-45; Luke 22: 25-26.
John 21: 15-17.
Matt. 25: 34-40.

D. He required the life of self-sacrifice as a test of discipleship.
Mark 8: 34-38. Parallel passages: Matt. 16: 24-26; Luke 9: 23-25.
John 15: 12-13.

E. He required a life of supreme loyalty to God.
Luke 4: 8. Parallel passage: Matt. 4: 10.
Matt. 22: 36-37. Parallel passage: Mark 12: 28-31.

6. *Jesus is said to have condemned war in revealing God as a universal Father.*

A. He revealed Him as a loving Father.
John 3: 16.
Matt. 5: 45.

Luke 11:11-13.
Luke 15:7, 10.

B. He portrayed Him as a forgiving Father.
Luke 15:11-32.
Luke 18:9-14.
Matt. 6:14.

C. He asserted that He was a redeeming Father.
John 3:14-17.
Matt. 18:12-14.

7. *Jesus is said to have condemned war in asserting that the individual is of infinite value.*
Matt. 12:11-12.
Luke 12:6-7. Parallel passage: Matt. 10:29-31.
Luke 12:24.
Matt. 25:40.

8. *Jesus is said to have condemned war in calling for a rich and abundant life for all.*
John 10:10b.
Luke 18:28-30. Parallel passages: Matt. 19:27-30. Mark 10:28-31.

9. *Jesus is said to have condemned war in establishing standards by which institutions, such as war, must be judged.*
Matt. 7:15-20. Parallel passage: Luke 6:43-44.

BIBLIOGRAPHY.

I. *Books which favor defensive war.*

A. From a religious standpoint:

What did Jesus really teach about War,
Edward Leigh Pell—Fleming H. Revell Co., N. Y. C.

Social Evolution and Development of Religion,
Carl K. Mahoney—Methodist Book Concern, N. Y. C.

Christ and the World at War,
Sermons by Twelve British Church Leaders—Pilgrim Press, Boston, Mass.

Church and College Denounce Pacifist Pledge,
The National Civic Federation—1 Madison Ave., N. Y. C.

The Copec Commission Reports, Vol. VIII; Christianity and War—The section in favor of defensive warfare—Longmans Green and Co., London, Eng.

B. For other reasons.

War of Defense is always Justifiable,
Joseph T. Cashman—National Security League, 25 W. 43d St., N. Y. C.

The Main Illusions of Pacifism,
G. G. Coulton—Bowes, Cambridge, Eng.

War Facts and Peace Problems,
Frothingham — National Security League, N. Y. C.

Fear God and Take Your Own Part,
Theodore Roosevelt—Geo. H. Doran & Co., N. Y. C.

II. *Books which oppose war.*

The Sword or the Cross,
Kirby Page—Christian Century Press, Chicago, Ill.

The Abolition of War,
Sherwood Eddy & Kirby Page—Geo. H. Doran & Co., N. Y. C.

Was Jesus a Patriot,
Kirby Page—Fellowship of Reconciliation.

The Basis of the Ethics of Jesus,
Richard Roberts—Fellowship of Reconciliation, 383 Bible House, N. Y. C.

War Inconsistent with the Religion of Jesus Christ,
David Low Dodge—Ginn & Co., Boston, Mass.

War as Viewed by Jesus and the Early Church,
Wilfred Wellock—The No More War Movement, 11 Doughty St., London, Eng. W. C. 1.

The Christ Method of Peace Making,
W. Evans Darby—Headley Brothers, Bishopsgate Street Without, E. C. London, Eng.

The Bible and Universal Peace,
George H. Gilbert—Funk-Wagnalls Co., N. Y. C.

The God of War,
Joseph J. Taylor—Fleming H. Revell Co., N. Y. C.

The Christian and War,
Joint authorship—McClelland & Stewart, Toronto, Canada.

The Copec Commission Reports, Vol. VIII: Christianity and War—Longmans, Green & Co., London, Eng.

Toward the Understanding of Jesus,
V. Simkovitch—Macmillan Co., N. Y. C.

Christianity and International Peace,
Charles E. Jefferson—T. Y. Crowell Co., N.Y.C.

The Christian Revolution,
Henry T. Hodgkin—Swarthmore Press, London, Eng.

The Untried Door,
Richard Roberts—The Woman's Press, N. Y. C.

The Christian Ideal,
W. E. Wilson—Swarthmore Press, London, Eng.

Christ or Mars,
Will Irwin—D. Appleton & Co., N. Y. C.

Why We Fail as Christians,
Robert Hunter—Macmillan Co., N. Y. C.

New Wars for Old,
John Haynes Holmes—Dodd, Mead & Co., N. Y. C.

The Early Christian Attitude to War,
C. J. Cadoux—Headley Bros., London, Eng.

Christ and War,
William E. Wilson—James Clark & Co., London, Eng.

A Service of Love in War Time,
Rufus Jones—Macmillan Co., N. Y. C.

Cyrus Pringles' Diary; the Record of a Quaker Conscience—Macmillan Co., N. Y. C.

Rebel Saints,
Mary Agnes Best—Harcourt, Brace & Co., N. Y. C.

III. *Books which deal with the causes, nature and consequences of war.*

The Great Illusion,
Norman Angell—Putnam's, N. Y. C.

War—Its Causes, Consequences and Cure,
Kirby Page—Geo. H. Doran, N. Y. C.

War—Its Nature, Cause and Cure,
G. Lowes Dickinson—Macmillan Co., N. Y. C.

Why Men Fight,
Bertrand Russell—Century Co., N. Y. C.

Shall It be Again,
John K. Turner—Huebsch, N. Y. C.

Dollars and World Peace,
Kirby Page—George H. Doran Co., N. Y. C.

Imperialism and World Politics,
Parker T. Moon—Macmillan Co., N. Y. C.

431 261

Biology of War,
G. F. Nicolai—Century Co., N. Y. C.

The Moral Damage of War,
Walter Walsh—Ginn & Co., N. Y. C.

The Challenge of War—An Economic Interpretation,
Norman Thomas—League for Industrial Democracy, 70 Fifth Avenue, N. Y. C.

Now It Can Be Told,
Philip Gibbs—Harper Bros., N. Y. C. and London.

More That Must Be Told,
Philip Gibbs—Harper Bros., N. Y. C. and London.

A Student in Arms,
Donald Hankey—E. P. Dutton & Co., N. Y. C.

Under Fire,
Henri Barbusse—E. P. Dutton & Co., N. Y. C.

Men in War,
Andreas Latzko—Boni & Liveright, N. Y. C.

War Myth in U. S. History,
C. H. Hamlin—Vanguard Press, N. Y. C.

IV. *Books which deal with methods and plans for the abolition of war.*

Peace and Bread,
Jane Addams—Macmillan Co., N. Y. C.

Newer Ideals of Peace,
Jane Addams—Macmillan Co., N. Y. C.

The Next Step,
Scott Nearing—N. S. Nearing, Ridgewood, N. J.

The Outlawry of War,
Charles C. Morrison—Willett, Clark & Colby, Chicago, Ill.

League or War,
Irving Fisher—Harper Bros., N. Y. C.

Non-Violent Coercion,
C. M. Case—The Century Co., N. Y. C.

Building International Goodwill,
World Alliance for International Friendship Through the Churches—Macmillan Co., N. Y. C.

The Christian Crusade for a Warless World.
Sidney L. Gulick—Federal Council of Churches, N. Y. C.

An American Peace Policy,
Kirby Page—Geo. H. Doran & Co., N. Y. C.

International Problems and the Christian Way of Life,
The Inquiry—129 E. 52d St., N. Y. C.

The Search for Peace,
National Council of the Protestant Episcopal Church, 281 Fourth Avenue, N. Y. C.

Christian Fellowship Among the Nations,
Jerome Davis and Roy B. Chamberlain—Pilgrim Press, Boston.

War as an Instrument of National Policy,
James T. Shotwell—Harcourt, Brace & Co.

Law or War,
Lucia Ames Mead—Doubleday-Doran.

Additional copies of this pamphlet may be had at the following rates:

Single copy	15c
10 or more in one package	10c each
100 or more in one package	$7.50 per 100

Copies and any further information that may be desired in regard to bibliography or use of the course may be obtained from the Commission on the Church and Social Service of the Federal Council of Churches, 105 East 22d Street, New York City.